Contents

asparagus

Asparagus is a tasty vegetable you can buy in a store. Eating asparagus helps you stay healthy.

4

ABCs
at the Store

Rebecca Rissman

Chicago, Illinois

www.capstonepub.com
Visit our website to find out
more information about
Heinemann-Raintree books.

To order:

☎ Phone 800-747-4992

💻 Visit www.capstonepub.com
to browse our catalog and order online.

Edited by Dan Nunn and Rebecca Rissman
Designed by Joanna Hinton-Malivoire
Picture research by Ruth Blair
Originated by Capstone Global Library Ltd
Production by Alison Parsons

Library of Congress Cataloging-in-Publication Data
Rissman, Rebecca.
ABCs at the store / Rebecca Rissman.
p. cm.—(Everyday alphabet)
Includes bibliographical references and index.
ISBN 978-1-4109-4729-1—ISBN 978-1-4109-4734-5 (pbk.) 1. English
language—Alphabet—Juvenile literature. 2. Stores, Retail—
Juvenile literature. I. Title.
PE1155.R57 2012
428.13—dc23   2011043700

Acknowledgments
We would like to thank the following for permission to reproduce
photographs: Dreamstime.com p. 9 (© Monkey Business Images);
Shutterstock pp. 4 (© Feng Yu), 5 (© atoss), 6 (© Studio DMM
Photography, Designs & Art), 7 (© Zayats Svetlana), 8 (© Inc), 10
(© Alexander Dashewsky), 11 (© Petrenko Andriy), 12 (© Elena
Elisseeva), 13 (© Rafa Irusta), 14 (© atoss), 15 (© Valentyn Volkov),
16 (© Peter zijlstra), 17 (© Andrjuss), 18 (© GeorgeS), 19 (©
Kamenetskiy Konstantin), 20 (© jreika), 21 (© Janet Faye Hastings),
22 (© Shmeliova Natalia), 23 (© valzan), 24 (© TerraceStudio),
25 (© liza1979), 26 (© Elena Schweitzer), 27 (© Mikus, Jo.), 28
(© Lepas), 29 (© atoss), 30 (© graja, © Michael Cocita), 31 (©
Valentyn Volkov, © Loskutnikov, © Tim Arbaev).

Cover photograph of food in a supermarket aisle reproduced with
permission of Shutterstock (© Hannamariah).

Every effort has been made to contact copyright holders of any
material reproduced in this book. Any omissions will be rectified in
subsequent printings if notice is given to the publisher.

Bb

bananas

Bananas are often green when you buy them. When bananas are ripe, they turn yellow.

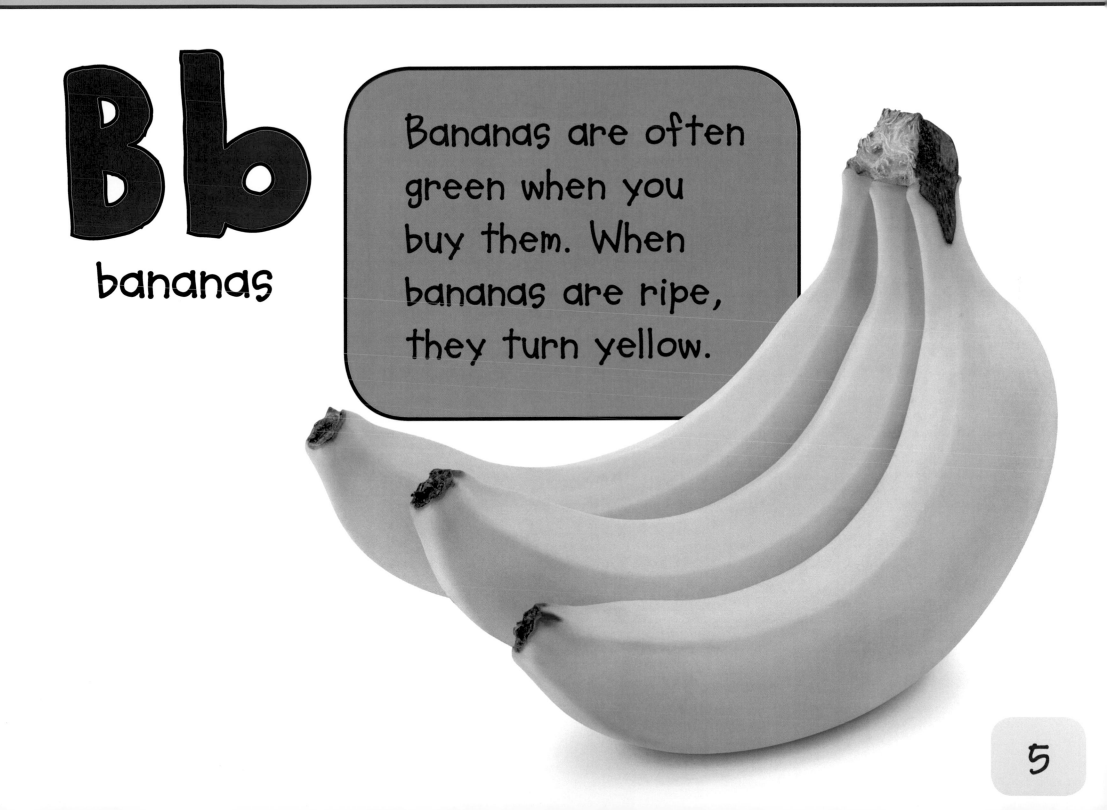

Cc
crayons

Colored crayons are great for drawing pictures. What picture can you draw?

Dd

doll

You can buy lots
of different dolls.
There are rag dolls,
baby dolls, tiny dolls,
and many more.

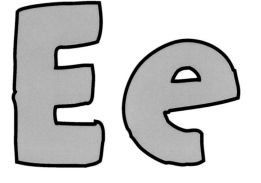

Ee

eggs

Hens lay eggs. Then the eggs are sold in boxes.

Ff

flour

Flour is used in baking. We use it to make bread, cookies, and cakes.

Gg

grapes

Grapes are fruit. You can buy green and purple grapes.

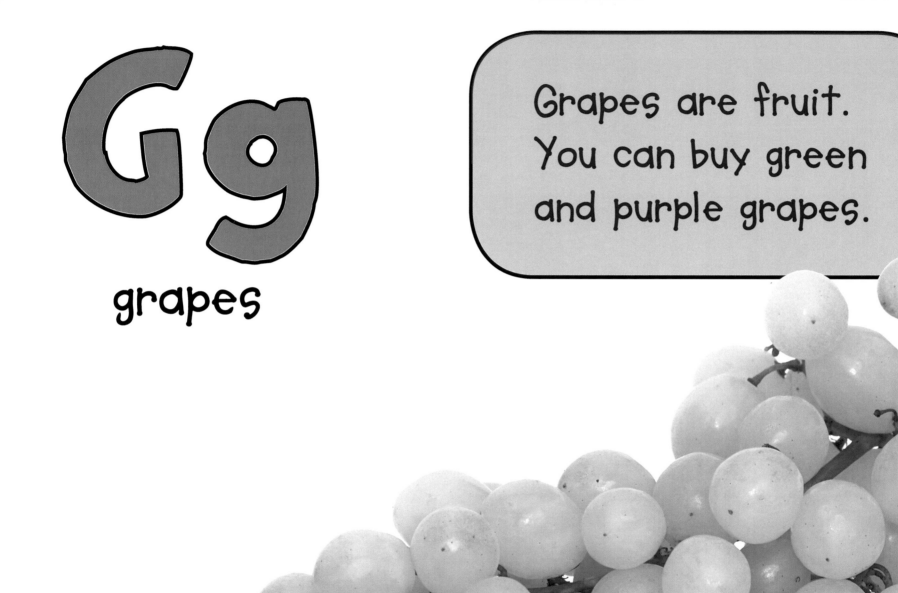

Hh

honey

Honey is made by bees! Stores sell it in jars. Honey tastes great on toast.

Ii

ice cream

Ice cream is made from milk. You can eat ice cream scoops on tasty cones.

Jj

juice

Juice can be made from oranges, apples, grapes, and many other fruits. Juice tastes great!

13

kiwifruit

Kiwifruit have brown, fuzzy skin, but their insides taste sweet!

Ll

lemons

Lemons are fruit that grow on trees. Lemons taste very sour!

15

M m

mangoes

Mangoes are fruit with a thick skin and a big seed. Mangoes taste very sweet.

Nn

nectarines

Nectarines are fruit with a large, hard seed. This is why they are sometimes called "stone fruit"!

Oo

oranges

Oranges are fruit
with a thick peel.
Oranges are juicy
and sweet.

Pp

potatoes

Potatoes are vegetables that grow under the ground. Chips are made from potatoes.

quiches

Quiches are egg pies! You can buy quiches at some stores to take home and eat.

Rr

raspberries

Raspberries are small red berries. They are very sweet and have many little seeds.

S s

shoes

Shoes are made in all shapes, sizes, and colors. You buy two shoes in a pair.

22

Tt

tomatoes

Tomatoes are round, red fruit. They are used to make pasta sauce, and ketchup.

23

Uu

umbrella

Don't forget your umbrella if you go shopping on a rainy day!

Vv

vegetables

Eating vegetables keeps you healthy. What are your favorite vegetables?

Ww

watermelons

Watermelons are large fruit. They have a thick green rind on the outside and red flesh on the inside.

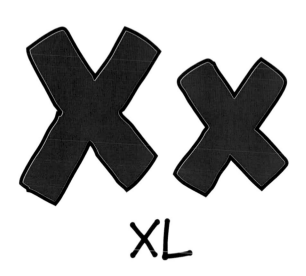

XL

T-shirts come in different sizes. XL stands for "extra large."

XL

XL

27

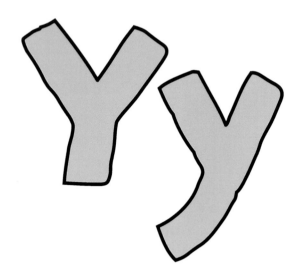

yogurt

Yogurt is a food made from milk. You can buy it in different flavors.

Zz

zucchinis

Zucchini is a type of squash. It is a yummy and healthy vegetable.

Find Your Own ABCs at the Store

Can you find your own ABCs at the store? How many different things beginning with each letter can you find? Here are some ideas to help you!

Cc

Pp

Index